This Notebook Belongs To

____

Made in the USA
Middletown, DE
26 January 2020

83757832R00068